France

The

 GW01454219

Activities by **Jenny** ~~Pereira~~ and **Kenneth Brodey**

Illustrated by **Giovanni Manna**

Editors: Rebecca Raynes, Mary Johnson
Design and art direction: Nadia Maestri
Computer graphics: Simona Corniola
Picture research: Laura Lagomarsino

© 2007   Black Cat Publishing,
            an imprint of Cideb Editrice, Genoa, Canterbury

Picture credits

Library of Congress, Print & Photographs Division: 5; Hulton Archive/Laura
Ronchi: 6, 90, 91; © The Salvation Army International Heritage Centre: 7; From
Picture Collection at Royal Holloway, University of London: 89; Victoria and
Albert Museum, London: 92

We would be happy to receive your comments and suggestions, and give you
any other information concerning our material.
editorial@blackcat-cideb.com
www.blackcat-cideb.com
www.cideb.it

CISQ **CISQCERT**
TEXTBOOKS AND
TEACHING MATERIALS
The quality of the publisher's
design, production and sales processes has
been certified to the standard of
UNI EN ISO 9001

ISBN 978-88-530-0690-5 Book
ISBN 978-88-530-0689-9 Book + audio CD/CD-ROM

Printed in Italy by Litoprint, Genoa

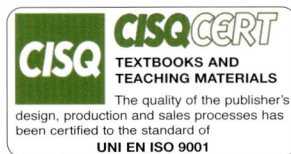

The CD contains an audio section (the recording of the text) and a CD-ROM section
(additional fun games and activities that practise the four skills).
– To listen to the recording, insert the CD into your CD player and it will play as
  normal. You can also listen to the recording on your computer, by opening your usual
  CD player program.
– If you put the CD directly into the CD-ROM drive, the software will open
  automatically.

SYSTEM REQUIREMENTS for CD-ROM	
PC: • Pentium III processor • Windows 98, 2000 or XP • 64 Mb RAM (128Mb RAM recommended) • 800x600 screen resolution 16 bit • 12X CD-ROM drive • Audio card with speakers or headphones	**Macintosh:** • Power PC G3 or above (G4 recommended) • Mac OS 10.1.5 • 128 Mb RAM free for the application
All the trademarks above are copyright.	

Contents

This story is recorded in full.

These symbols indicate the beginning and end of the extracts linked to the listening activities.

Frances Hodgson Burnett

Frances Hodgson Burnett (1849-1924) was born in Manchester, England. When she was sixteen years old, she and her family moved to Knoxville, Tennessee, USA. She wrote a lot of very popular books for children. Her most famous novel, *Little Lord Fauntleroy* (1886), started a fashion in velvet suits [1] for small boys!

The Secret Garden (1911) describes how two sad, lonely children find happiness by looking after an abandoned garden. This very popular story was filmed twice, in 1949 and 1993.

---

1. **velvet suits** : jackets and trousers made of a soft smooth material.

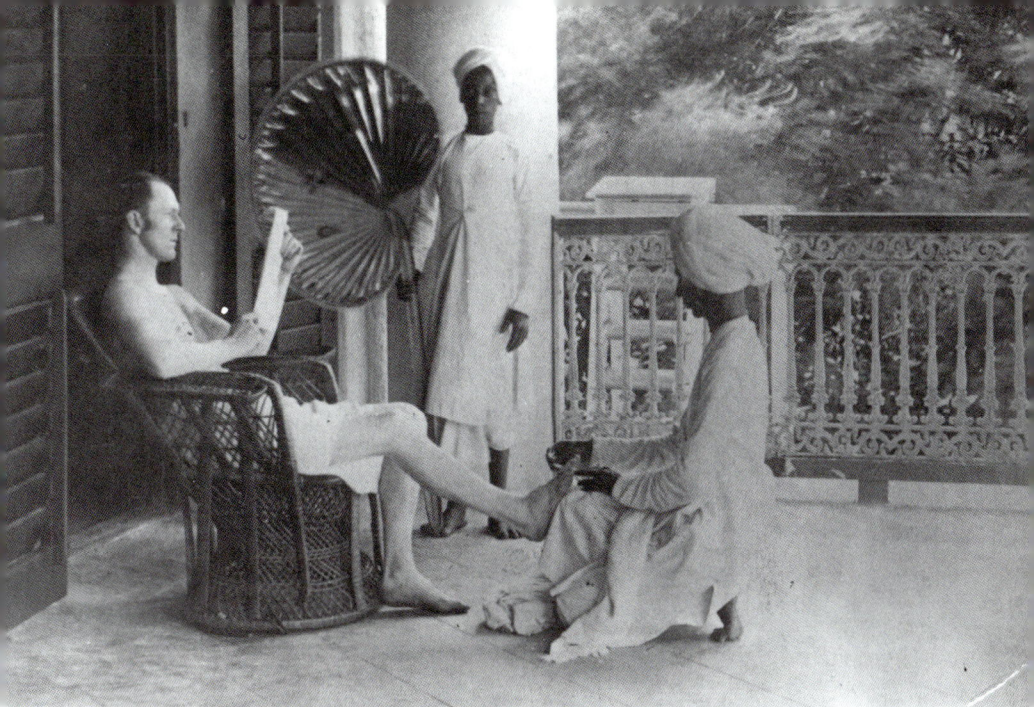

A British officer in India with his Indian servants. One has a fan to keep the officer cool while the other is cutting his toenails.

The World of The Secret Garden

At the time that Frances Hodgson Burnett wrote *The Secret Garden* in 1911, Britain controlled all of India.

Thousands of British people went to India to help govern the country. Many of them had a luxurious [1] lifestyle; Indian servants did everything for them but the British people were not always nice to them. The British children who lived in India were looked after by Indian nannies [2] who had to do everything that the children asked. So it was not surprising that some of these children became spoilt [3] and lazy.

---

1. **luxurious** : comfortable and expensive.
2. **nannies** : women who were paid to look after children.
3. **spoilt** : unpleasant because they got everything they wanted or asked for.

Back in Britain, things were similar for most children of rich families. They, too, were brought up by servants and governesses, and they only saw their parents for a short time each day.

Life was very different, however, for poor families. There were often ten or more children living with their parents in small houses with only one or two bedrooms. There was not always enough food for everyone and clothes were passed down from the older children to the younger ones. Children started work at an early age to earn money to buy food and clothes for the rest of the family.

Poor children in London queuing for breakfast at a Salvation Army hostel. The Salvation Army, a Christian organisation, was started in London in 1865 to give food and help to the poor and hungry.

1 Comprehension check

Read the sentences and decide if they are true (T) or false (F). Then correct the false ones.

		T	F
1	When Frances Hodgson Burnett wrote *The Secret Garden* India controlled all of Britain.	☐	☐
2	Thousands of British people went to live in India.	☐	☐
3	Many British people lived very well there.	☐	☐
4	British children looked after Indian nannies.	☐	☐
5	Things were very different in Britain for rich families.	☐	☐
6	Rich children in Britain saw their parents a lot.	☐	☐
7	In poor families there were usually fewer children than in rich families.	☐	☐
8	Poor families lived in houses with no bedroom.	☐	☐
9	Younger children wore old clothes.	☐	☐
10	Poor children started work after finishing school.	☐	☐

....

....

....

....

....

....

....

2 Vocabulary

Match the following words (1-5) with their definitions (A-E).

1	☐	govern	A	care for
2	☐	look after	B	receive money for work you do
3	☐	lazy	C	control
4	☐	governess	D	not wanting to work
5	☐	earn	E	woman who lives with a family and teaches the children

Before you read

PET ❶ **Listening**

Listen to the first part of Chapter One. For each question, put a tick (✓) in the correct box.

1 Because Mary was often ill she was

- **A** ☐ spoilt and rude.
- **B** ☐ thin and sad.
- **C** ☐ rude and thin.

2 Mary spent most of her time with her

- **A** ☐ mother.
- **B** ☐ father.
- **C** ☐ nanny.

3 Mary was angry because

- **A** ☐ there were strange cries.
- **B** ☐ no one came to see her.
- **C** ☐ the house was silent.

4 Mary was sent to

- **A** ☐ Yorkshire.
- **B** ☐ London.
- **C** ☐ India.

5 Why didn't Mrs Medlock like Mary?

- **A** ☐ Because Mary was rude.
- **B** ☐ Because Mrs Medlock didn't like anyone.
- **C** ☐ Because Mrs Medlock didn't like children.

6 During the journey to Yorkshire Mrs Medlock told Mary about

- **A** ☐ the house and Mr Craven.
- **B** ☐ the moor.
- **C** ☐ India.

CHAPTER ONE

A Spoilt [1] Little Girl

ary Lennox was spoilt, rude and had a bad temper. [2] Because she was often ill she was thin and had a sad face. She complained [3] a lot. No one liked her at all.

This was not really Mary's fault. She lived in India with her mother and father, but she did not see her parents very often. Mary's father was busy with his work and her mother was a very beautiful woman who loved parties and was not interested in her small daughter. She left Mary in the care of an Indian nanny, [4] called an ayah. Her ayah allowed Mary to do anything she wanted because she didn't want Mary to cry and make her mother angry. So Mary soon became a spoilt and unpleasant young girl.

1. **spoilt** : unpleasant because she got everything she wanted or asked for.
2. **had a bad temper** : became angry quickly.
3. **complained** : said she wasn't satisfied or happy.
4. **nanny** : woman paid to look after children.

9

The Secret Garden

When Mary was nine years old she woke up one hot morning and felt that there was something wrong. She heard strange cries and shouts and the sound of feet outside her door, but no one came to see her. She went back to sleep.

Later, when Mary woke up again, the house was silent. She heard nothing. Mary was angry because no one came to bring her food or to dress her. Suddenly her door opened and two Englishmen came in. Mary looked at them angrily.

'Why has everyone forgotten me?' she asked. 'Where's my ayah? Where is everyone?'

'Poor little girl,' said one of the men. 'There's nobody here.'

That is how Mary discovered that her mother and father were dead and that the servants were dead, too, because of a terrible disease. That was why the house was so silent. Mary Lennox was completely alone.

There was no one in India to look after Mary, so she was sent to England to live with her uncle, Mr Craven, who lived in a big house in Yorkshire [1] called Misselthwaite Manor.

Mrs Medlock, her uncle's housekeeper, [2] met Mary in London. As soon as she saw her, Mary didn't like Mrs Medlock. But this was nothing new, because Mary didn't like anyone.

Mrs Medlock didn't like Mary. She thought that the little girl was bad-tempered, rude and plain [3] — and she was right.

During the long train journey to Yorkshire, Mrs Medlock told Mary about the house where she was going to live. It seemed very large and gloomy, [4] and it was on the edge of a moor. [5]

---

1. **Yorkshire** : a region in the north of England.
2. **housekeeper** : the most important woman servant in a rich house.
3. **plain** : not pretty.
4. **gloomy** : dark and depressing.
5. **moor** : a large area of wild, open land.

A Spoilt Little Girl

'There's nothing for you to do there, and your uncle is not interested in you,' said Mrs Medlock. 'He's got a crooked [1] back. He was an unpleasant young man until he got married.'

Mary listened more carefully now. She did not know that her uncle was married.

'His wife was very pretty, and he loved her very much. When she died he became even stranger,' Mrs Medlock said.

'Oh, did she die?' asked Mary.

'Yes, and now he doesn't like anybody. He's away most of the time, so you must look after yourself.'

It was dark and raining when they got out of the train. They travelled to the house in a carriage, [2] but Mary couldn't see anything because of the rain and the dark.

'What's a moor?' Mary asked.

1. **crooked** : [krʊkɪd] : not straight.   2. **carriage** :

'It's miles [1] and miles of land,' replied Mrs Medlock. 'Very little grows on it, and nothing lives there except ponies and sheep.'

At last, the carriage stopped outside a large house. A butler [2] opened a heavy wooden door.

'Take her to her room,' he said to Mrs Medlock. 'Mr Craven doesn't want to see her. He's going to London tomorrow.'

Mrs Medlock took Mary upstairs and along many corridors [3] to a room with a fire burning in it and food on the table.

'Well, here you are,' said Mrs Medlock. 'This is where you're going to live. This room and the one next to it is where you must stay. You can't go into the other parts of the house. Don't forget that.'

Mary Lennox felt very lonely.

1. **miles** : a mile is equal to 1.6 kilometres.
2. **butler** : the most important man servant in a rich house.
3. **corridors** : passages in a building.

Go back to the text

PET ① **Comprehension check**

For each question, mark the letter next to the correct answer — A, B, C or D.

1   Who liked Mary Lennox?
   A ☐ Mrs Medlock
   B ☐ her ayah
   C ☐ her mother
   D ☐ no one

2   Who looked after Mary?
   A ☐ her ayah
   B ☐ her mother
   C ☐ her father
   D ☐ no one

3   Where did Mary's uncle live?
   A ☐ Yorkshire
   B ☐ London
   C ☐ India
   D ☐ Devonshire

4   What was the name of Mary's uncle?
   A ☐ Mr Medlock
   B ☐ Mr Craven
   C ☐ Mr Lennox
   D ☐ Mr Misselthwaite

5   Who was Mrs Medlock?
   A ☐ Mary's new nanny
   B ☐ Mary's aunt
   C ☐ Mary's teacher
   D ☐ Mr Craven's housekeeper

6   What happened to Mr Craven after his wife died?
   A ☐ He went to live on the moor.
   B ☐ He became even stranger than when he was a young man.
   C ☐ He got a crooked back.
   D ☐ He became rich.

2 **What do you think?**

Would you like Mary to be your friend? Why/why not? Do you think that Mary was happy to go to Misselthwaite Manor?

....

....

....

....

....

3 **Adjectives**

Match the adjectives in column A with their opposites in column B.

A	B
mean	young
rich	bad
plain	stupid
clever	sad
hard-working	poor
good	pretty
old	lazy
happy	generous

4 **Describing people**

People thought that Mary was 'spoilt, rude and had a bad temper'. Complete these sentences. Add the names of famous people, or of people you know.

1   .... is kind, generous and friendly.

2   .... is young, pretty and rich.

3   .... is strong, handsome and brave.

4   .... is intelligent, hard-working and successful.

5 Listening

PET

The beginning of Chapter One talks about a little girl named Mary Lennox and her life in India.

Listen to the text and for each question, fill in the missing information in the numbered space.

Mary's Life in India

Family

Mary's father was always busy with (**1**) ....

Mary's mother loved (**2**) ....

What Mary was like

Mary always did what (**3**) ....

She was a spoilt and (**4**) .... child.

Why Mary left India

The house was silent because Mary's parents and the servants were (**5**) ....

This happened when Mary was (**6**) .... years old.

T: GRADE 4

6 Topic – Houses

Mary has just arrived at Misselthwaite Manor — a very large gloomy house. Bring to class two pictures of different types of houses and use the following questions to help you talk about them.

1 What types of houses are they?

2 Describe them.

3 Now compare them.

4 Which one do you like the most? Why?

5 Which one do you like the least?

6 Now describe your house. Is it similar to one in the pictures?

7 **Name the objects**

What are the numbered objects? Use your dictionary to help.

Example: *Number 1 is a bed.*

Number 2 ....

Number 3 ....

Number 4 ....

Number 5 ....

Number 6 ....

Number 7 ....

Number 8 ....

Number 9 ....

Number 10 ....

Number 11 ....

Number 12 ....

PET ⑧ Write a letter

Pretend you are Mrs Medlock and this is part of a letter you have received from your friend who works in another big Yorkshire manor.

> I also have to look after two small children. I like them both very much. Do you have to look after children too? Do you like them?

Write your letter in about 100 words.

Say

- who Mary Lennox is
- why she came to Misselthwaite Manor
- what she is like
- if you like her

⑨ Summary

Put the following sentences in the correct order.

A ☐ They travelled by train to Yorkshire.
B ☐ She was sent to England to live with her uncle.
C ☐ Mary's uncle didn't want to see her.
D ☐ Mary was met in London by her uncle's housekeeper.
E ☐ It was dark and rainy when they arrived at Misselthwaite Manor.
F ☐ Mary Lennox was spoilt, rude and had a bad temper.
G ☐ Everyone in the house, except for Mary, died of a terrible disease.
H ☐ She lived in India with her mother and father.

Now write out the sentences so that you have your own summary of the story so far.

India

Mary Lennox was living in India because her father worked for the British government. Why was he there? To answer this question, we must look at the history of India.

In 1526 the Moguls – Muslim people from Mongolian and Turkish origins – came to India. They took power from the Hindu people who already lived there. In the next 200 years of the Mogul Empire [1] some beautiful art and buildings were created.

India became a rich country. In the 17th century some European counties – Portugal, Britain, France and Holland – created companies to buy and sell things in India. But soon these companies wanted more than business. They wanted political power, too, and used force and armies to get this power.

The British East India Company became the most powerful of these companies, and had a lot of soldiers in India. In 1803 they took Delhi, the Mogul capital, but the Indian soldiers who worked for the East India Company tried to fight against it in 1857. The 'Indian Mutiny', [2] as it was called, did not succeed. The British government sent a lot of soldiers and took control of all of India, which then became part of the British Empire.

So, in 1858, the British Raj started in India. 'Raj' is a word from Hindi (the Indian language with most speakers) which means the control of a country by a king or queen. Queen Victoria of Britain was made 'Empress of India' in 1877, and during the Raj (1858-1947) people like

1. **Empire** : an empire is a number of countries that are all controlled by the government of just one country (another example from history is the Roman Empire).
2. **mutiny** : when a group of people, usually soldiers, decide not to follow the orders of the person in control.

British people during the Raj walking in a park in India *c*. 1915.

Mary Lennox's father went to work in India.

But most Indians wanted independence. In 1920 the great pacifist [1] Mahatma Gandhi (1869-1948) started a campaign [2] for independence. Finally, in 1947, Britain created two independent states: Pakistan in the north, where most people were Muslim, and India, where most people were Hindu. In the first weeks of independence, however, over a million people were killed when Muslims and Hindus attacked each other.

In modern India you can see the effect of the British Raj in large public buildings, the education system and the wide use of English. India today is the world's largest democracy with a population of 1.1 billion (only China has a bigger population) and an area of 3.1 million square kilometres. It is a country of variety: apart from Hindi

1. **pacifist** : this person believes that violence is wrong: he/she acts in a peaceful way to try to get what he/she wants.
2. **campaign** : a number of activities, over a period time, to try to get political changes.

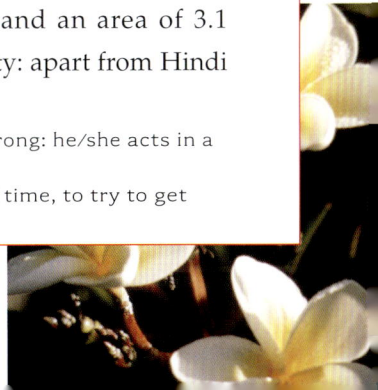

The Taj Mahal, near Agra in northern India, finished in about 1648. The Mogul emperor Shah Jahan built it as a place to bury his favourite wife, Mumtaz Mahal, who was the mother of 14 of his children.

and English there are another 26 official languages. It is also a country of contrasts: many people outside the cities are poor and uneducated, but India is a nuclear power, with a big information technology industry and the biggest film industry in the world.

1 Comprehension check

Look at the words and names below. Put them into the order in which they appear in the text. Can you do it from memory? Then prepare to say a sentence about each of them. Try to use a date if possible.

A ☐ Victoria   B ☐ Pakistan   C ☐ Mogul

D ☐ East India Company   E ☐ Hindi   F ☐ Gandhi

G ☐ Indian Mutiny

Before you read

1 **Listening**

PET

Listen to the beginning of Chapter Two. For each question, put a tick (✓) in the correct box.

1   Mary woke up when the housemaid came into her room to
   A ☐ bring her breakfast.
   B ☐ help Mary get dressed.
   C ☐ light the fire.

2   In India, Mary spoke to her servants only to
   A ☐ give them orders.
   B ☐ say 'Please' or 'Thank you'.
   C ☐ ask them for help.

3   How many shillings a week does Martha's father earn?
   A ☐ six
   B ☐ sixty
   C ☐ sixteen

4   How old is Martha's brother Dickon?
   A ☐ two
   B ☐ twelve
   C ☐ thirteen

5   The closed garden was
   A ☐ Martha's
   B ☐ Mr Craven's
   C ☐ Mr Craven's wife's

6   Mary thought that the gardens looked ugly because
   A ☐ gardens in India are much more colourful and interesting.
   B ☐ she did not like plants.
   C ☐ it was winter and the trees had no leaves and there were no flowers.

CHAPTER TWO

Mary Visits the Gardens

he next morning, Mary woke up when a young housemaid[1] came into her room to light the fire. Her name was Martha, and she talked to Mary while she worked.

Mary didn't understand servants who were friendly. In India she spoke to servants only to give them orders. She never said 'Please' or 'Thank you'. Once, she even slapped[2] her ayah's face when she was angry with her. But for some reason she knew that she must not behave in this way with Martha.

At first Mary didn't listen to Martha, but then she began to like the sound of her friendly voice.

'You should see all my little brothers and sisters in our little

---

1. **housemaid** : a woman servant who worked in a rich house.
2. **slapped** : hit with the palm of her hand.

cottage on the moor,' Martha said. 'There are twelve of us, and my father only earns sixteen shillings [1] a week. It's hard for my mother to feed them all. The fresh air on the moor makes them strong and healthy. Dickon is twelve. He's always out on the moor. He's good with animals. He's tamed [2] a wild pony.

'Go and look at the gardens,' Martha said. 'There's not much growing now, but they're lovely in summer.' She stopped for a moment, and then said quietly, 'One of the gardens is locked up. It was locked up ten years ago.'

'Why?' asked Mary.

'Mr Craven locked it up after his wife died. It was her garden. He locked the door, made a hole in the ground and buried [3] the key.'

The enormous grounds [4] of Misselthwaite Manor were divided by high walls into many gardens. In some there were flowers, trees and fountains. Vegetables grew in others. Doors opened from some gardens into other gardens.

Because it was winter, the trees were bare and no flowers grew. Mary thought that the gardens all looked very empty and ugly.

After some time an old man came through one of the doors. He had an unfriendly face and didn't seem at all pleased to see Mary.

'Can I go through that door?' Mary asked.

'If you like,' he replied. 'There's nothing to see.'

---

1. **shillings** : eighty pence in modern British money (there were 20 shillings in a pound).
2. **tamed** : made it not afraid of people.
3. **buried** : [berɪd] : put in the ground and covered with earth.
4. **grounds** : the land around a house.

Mary hoped that she might find the door to the locked garden. She tried a lot of doors, but they all opened easily. Then she noticed one wall that was covered in ivy,[1] but it seemed to have no door in it. She could see tall trees behind the ivy-covered wall. A robin[2] on a high branch started to sing. She stopped to listen, and it seemed that the little bird was calling to her. His happy song brought a small smile to her sad face.

The old man continued working. He didn't speak to Mary until at last she said, 'There's a garden over there without a door.'

'What garden?' he asked angrily.

'On the other side of the wall,' she answered. 'I saw a robin in the trees over there.'

The old man stopped working, and to Mary's surprise he smiled. He looked quite different when he smiled. He whistled[3] very quietly. Then a wonderful thing happened. There was a sound of wings,[4] and the robin came down next to the man's foot.

'Here he is,' the old man laughed quietly. 'He always comes to me when I whistle. Isn't he a nice little bird?'

The robin moved about, pecking[5] at the earth. The gardener, whose name was Ben Weatherstaff, continued working. 'He's the only friend I've got,' he said.

'I've never had any friends,' said Mary sadly.

---

1. **ivy** : a climbing plant.

2. **robin** :

3. **whistled** : made a musical sound with his mouth.

4. **wings** : part of a bird used for flying.

5. **pecking** : using its beak to look for things.

25

The Secret Garden

Ben stopped working and looked at Mary.

'You and I are the same, then,' he said to her. 'We're not good-looking, and we're as unpleasant as we look.'

It was the first time that Mary ever thought about her angry face and bad temper and she felt embarrassed. But at that moment the robin's song made her look towards an apple tree, where he was sitting now.

Ben Weatherstaff laughed.

'Why did he do that?' asked Mary.

'He's decided to be your friend,' replied Ben. 'He likes you.'

'Me?' said Mary, and she moved quietly towards the apple tree and looked up.

'Do you want to be my friend?' she said gently to the robin, as if she was speaking to a boy or a girl.

'Well, well, well,...' said Ben quietly, 'You said that like a real child instead of a little old woman. You said it almost like Dickon when he talks to his wild things on the moor.'

The robin flew over the wall.

'There must be a door to that garden,' Mary said.

'There's no door that you can find,' Ben said angrily, 'and in any case, it's none of your business!' [1] And then the gardener turned around and walked away without saying goodbye.

1. **it's none of your business** : it does not concern you.

Go back to the text

PET **1** **Comprehension check**

Decide if each statement is correct or incorrect.
If it is correct, mark A. If it is not correct, mark B.

A B

1   Mary understood that she must not be rude to Martha.

2   Martha's brother was always outside.

3   Misselthwaite had many gardens.

4   The old man was very happy to see Mary.

5   Mr Craven's wife died ten years ago.

6   Mary found the garden with the locked door.

7   The robin came when the old man whistled.

8   Mary had no friends in India.

9   Mary asked the old man to be her friend.

10 The old man became angry because Mary wanted
    to find the door to the locked garden.

Now correct the incorrect statements in exercise 1.

....

....

....

....

2 **Self-discovery**

Answer the following questions.

1   What did Ben Weatherstaff help Mary to discover about herself?

2   How did this make her feel?

3   In Ben's opinion how did Mary usually talk?

4   How did she talk to the robin?

3 The gardens of Misselthwaite Manor

There were flower gardens, tree gardens and vegetable gardens in the grounds of Misselthwaite Manor.

Look at the words in the box and put them into the correct gardens — vegetable words into the vegetable garden, flower words into the flower garden and tree words into the tree garden. Use your dictionary to help you.

> oak   rose   carrot   elm   ash   pea   pansy   daisy   sycamore
>
> sunflower   potato   turnip   buttercup
>
> plane   swede   runner bean   carnation

1 ....
....
....
....

2 oak ....
....
....
....

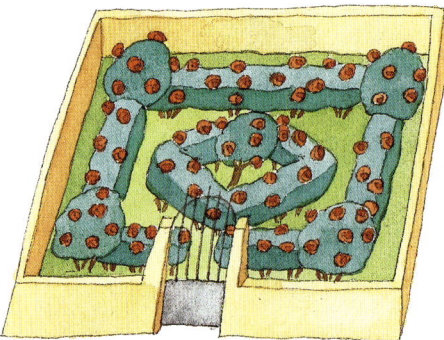

3 ....
....
....
....

4 **Opposites**

Write down the opposites of the words below. You can find them all in Chapter Two.

1   easy ....
2   weak ....
3   ill ....
4   bad ....
5   tiny ....

6   full ....
7   beautiful ....
8   sad ....
9   terrible ....
10 tame ....

Before you read

1 **Listening**

Listen to the beginning of Chapter Three. You will hear a conversation between Mary and Martha about the locked garden and Martha's brother Dickon. Decide if each sentence is correct or incorrect. If it is correct put a tick (✓) in the box under A for YES. If it is not correct, put a (✓) in the box under B for NO.

		A YES	B NO
1	The locked garden was Mr Craven's.	☐	☐
2	Mrs Craven died after falling from a tree in the locked garden.	☐	☐
3	Mary thought she heard someone crying.	☐	☐
4	Mary liked staying inside when the weather was bad.	☐	☐
5	Martha's brother went outside even when the weather was bad.	☐	☐
6	Martha's brother had a crow and a fox.	☐	☐

2 Now read the beginning of the chapter and correct those sentences that are not correct.

CHAPTER THREE

....

....

Crying in the Night

ary began to like her life at Misselthwaite Manor. Every morning after breakfast she went outside and spent most of the day in the grounds. The cold wind made her cheeks[1] pink, and each evening she ate all of her food. After dinner she liked sitting near the fire and talking to Martha.

'Why does Mr Craven hate the locked garden?' Mary asked once.

'It was Mrs Craven's garden. She loved it. She and Mr Craven looked after the flowers together. No gardeners were allowed in.'

'But what happened?' Mary asked.

'There was an old tree in the garden with a branch like a seat. She often sat there, reading and talking. One day the branch broke and she fell. She was injured so badly that she died. That's

1. **cheek** :

why Mr Craven hates the garden. He doesn't allow anyone to talk about it.'

Mary rarely felt sorry for anyone, but now she understood how unhappy her uncle must be.

The wind blew around the house, and the doors and windows banged. Mary listened and through the noise she thought that she heard a child crying.

'Can you hear someone crying?' she asked Martha.

Martha suddenly looked confused.

'No,' she answered, 'It's only the wind or the servant who works in the kitchen. She's got toothache, poor girl; perhaps she's crying.'

Then Martha left the room quickly.

The next day it rained. Mary was bored and complained to Martha that she had nothing to do.

'On a day like this at home, we all try to do things indoors,' Martha said. 'That is, all of us except Dickon. He goes out on the moor in all kinds of weather. He brought home a fox cub[1] that he found. He's got a crow,[2] too, called Soot.'

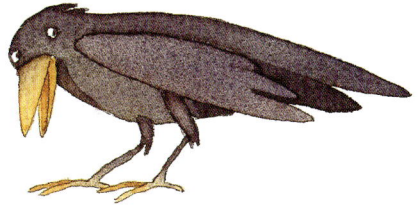

When Martha left her alone, Mary decided to explore the house. She went quietly along corridors and up and down stairs. In the silence of the house she heard again the sound of a child crying. She stopped to listen at a door, but then another door opened and Mrs Medlock came out. 'What are you doing here?' she said, and she took Mary by the arm and pulled her away. 'Get back to your room at once!'

---

1. **fox cub** : baby fox.   2. **crow** :

'I didn't know which way to go, and then I heard someone crying,' said Mary.

'You didn't hear anything,' said Mrs Medlock. 'Go back to your room, or I'll tell Mr Craven that you refused to do what I told you to do.'

But Mary still wanted to know what the sound of crying was.

Soon the storm passed. 'Wait until the sun shines: the moor looks better then,' said Martha.

'I'd like to see your cottage on the moor, and meet your mother,' said Mary.

'You'll like my mother when you meet her,' Martha said. 'She's kind and good-tempered and works hard. When it's my day off [1] and I can go home and see her, I'm very happy.'

'And I'd like to meet Dickon,' said Mary.

'Yes, you'll like him, too,' Martha said. 'Everyone likes Dickon.'

'No one likes me,' said Mary, sadly.

'Maybe that's because you don't like yourself,' laughed Martha.

'I've never thought of that,' said Mary.

Martha laughed again and left Mary. It was her day off and she went home across the moor to help her mother with the washing.

It wasn't raining now, so Mary went to the gardens. Ben Weatherstaff was there.

'Spring's coming,' he said. 'The plants are growing in the earth. Soon you'll see crocuses and daffodils.' [2]

---

1. **day off** : the day in the week when she doesn't work.
2. **crocuses and daffodils** : spring flowers.

The Secret Garden

Mary saw the robin on a wall covered with ivy. He flew down to her feet and tried to find a worm[1] in the earth. Suddenly, Mary saw an old, rusty[2] key.

'Perhaps it was buried for ten years,' she said to herself. 'And, perhaps it's the key to the garden,' she thought, putting it into her pocket. 'If I can find the door, then I can go inside and see it. It can become my garden!'

The next morning, Martha told Mary all about her day at home. 'Mother has sent you a present,' she said. She took out a skipping rope[3] and showed Mary how to skip.

'Your mother's very kind,' Mary said. She wondered[4] how Martha's mother could find enough money to buy her the skipping rope: she had a lot of children who needed food and clothes.

Mary skipped all the time, and the more she skipped, the stronger she grew. Her cheeks became red, and her plain face started to look almost pretty.

One day, as Mary was watching the robin in the garden, a wonderful thing happened. To Mary it was almost like magic. The wind blew some of the ivy on the wall to one side and, under the leaves, she saw a door. She remembered that she had the key in her pocket. She tried it in the lock; at first it didn't move, but then she turned it. The next moment, she was standing inside the secret garden.

For Mary it was a lovely and mysterious place. It was

1. **worm** :
2. **rusty** : covered in a reddish-brown substance.
3. **skipping rope** :
4. **wondered** : asked herself.

The Secret Garden

overgrown [1] and untidy, but she could see plants starting to come up through the earth. She pulled weeds [2] away to make space for the spring flowers to grow.

'Now they can breathe,' she thought. Then she said quietly to herself, 'I am the first person to speak in this garden for ten years.'

Time passed quickly as Mary took out the weeds and dead grass. Soon it was time to go back to the house for her dinner.

Mary wanted to tell Martha her secret, but she knew that this was not a good idea. They might not allow her to go into the secret garden again, so instead she said, 'I would like a little garden to grow things in.'

'Yes! That's exactly what you need to keep you busy,' said Martha. 'I'll ask Dickon to bring some garden tools [3] and some seeds [4] to plant.'

Mary worked with her hands each day in the secret garden. She was careful; she didn't want Ben Weatherstaff to see where she went. But Ben noticed a change in her. One day he said, 'The fresh air is good for you. You're less thin, and your skin is less pale.'

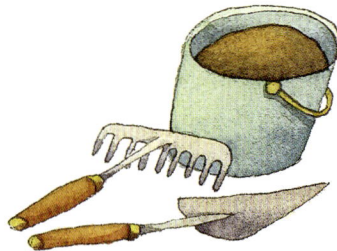

1. **overgrown** : covered in plants that people haven't cut.
2. **weeds** : wild plants that people don't want in gardens.
3. **tools** : things that you work with.
4. **seeds** : what new plants grow from.

Go back to the text

1 Comprehension check

Answer the questions.

1 Who looked after the garden before it was locked?
2 Who, according to Martha, was crying?
3 What did Mrs Medlock do when she found Mary exploring the house?
4 What was Martha's mother like?
5 Why, according to Martha, did nobody like Mary?
6 What did Mary find?
7 How did Mary discover the door to the secret garden?
8 Why didn't Mary tell Martha about the secret garden?

2 Changes

1 How is Mary changing physically?
2 Who is Mary sorry for? How does this show us that Mary is changing?
3 What does Mary wonder when she receives the skipping rope from Martha? How does this show us that Mary has changed since her arrival at Misselthwaite Manor?

3 Why is a little girl like a garden?

1 How does the author describe the garden when we first see it?
2 How does the author describe Mary when we first meet her?
3 Why is the garden in that condition?
4 Why was Mary in that condition?
5 Why is Mary beginning to change?
6 Why is the garden beginning to change?
7 What does Mary think of the garden when she first sees it?
8 What do you think Martha and her mother think about Mary?

He goes out on the moor in all types of weather

In English there are two principal present tenses: the Present Simple and the Present Continuous. Often, we use the Present Simple to describe what we do generally, and the Present Continuous to describe what is happening while we are speaking. Look at these examples.

- *Mary **works** in the locked garden on nice days.*
- *Mary **is working** in the locked garden. (It is a nice, sunny day today.)*
- *Mr Weatherstaff **speaks** with a Yorkshire accent.*
- *Mr Weatherstaff **is speaking** with Mary about the robin.*

Also, in English some verbs are not generally used in the Present Continuous or other Continuous tenses. Here are some of them:

feel, hear, see, notice, like, hate, prefer, want, agree, believe, forget, know, think, understand, need, have.

4 **Present Simple and Present Continuous**

Put the verbs in brackets in the Present Simple or Present Continuous according to the context.

0 Today is a beautiful day. The birds .are singing.. (*sing*), and the sun is shining..... (*shine*).

1 .... (*you/see*) that door? That is the door to the locked garden.

2 Martha .... (*not/work*). Today is a holiday and she is with her family.

3 I .... (*understand*) French perfectly. I lived in Paris for ten years.

4 (*Mrs Medlock discovers Mary in front of a locked door*) Mrs Medlock: 'What .... (*you/do*) here?'

5 Can you hear? A robin .... (*sing*) on the wall of the locked garden.

6 Mary .... (*feel*) sorry for her uncle.

7 Martha brought Mary a skipping rope. Now every morning Mary .... (*skip*) rope in the garden.

8 Mary is not in the house. She .... (*pull*) up weeds in the garden.

9 I know it is raining, but I .... (*want*) to go out on the moor with Dickon.

10 John: 'Philip, what .... (*you/do*)?' Philip: 'I'm a gardener.'

5 **What is Mary doing?**

Look at the pictures and complete the sentences below with the correct verb in the Present Continuous.

put on   eat   meet   go (x2)

1 Mary ....
into the garden.

2 Mary ....
an apple.

3 Mary .... to
bed.

4 Mary .... Dickon.

5 Mary .... her hat.

39

British Gardens

When Mary Lennox starts to love gardens and gardening, [1] she becomes a nicer person. She also becomes more 'British'. Most British people enjoy gardens and green spaces. You can see this in London: it has eight big parks and many smaller ones, and has more green space than any other city of its size in the world.

The gardens of the big country houses of the British upper classes show different fashions from different periods. Gardens, like

A typically British garden at Great Maytham Hall, in Kent, south-east England. On the left there is a border (many plants very near to each other at the side of a garden). There is a path for walking on and a large, flat area of grass, called a lawn. Frances Burnett, who loved gardening, lived here from 1898 to 1907.

1. **gardening** : working in a garden.

Vegetables at the Chelsea Flower Show.

buildings and clothes, were made according to the fashions of historical periods.

In the 18th century a 'British' fashion in gardens was created. Gardens in France, Italy and Spain were very organised, different from the natural world: they had plants, flowers and paths in straight lines. The gardens of big British houses in the 18th century became much more natural: they didn't have straight lines; they had a lot of grass; they had natural-looking lakes instead of rectangular ponds. [1] They were called 'landscape gardens'. [2]

In the Victorian period (1837-1901) it became fashionable to plant a lot of colourful flowers very near to each other: these areas are called 'flowerbeds'. In this period, too, a lot of parks, public gardens and green spaces were created for the public [3] to enjoy.

Today, parks and the gardens of the big country houses, many of which are open to the public, are very popular. But ordinary British people also like their own gardens! Gardening is very popular in the media. The BBC started the first radio programme for gardeners in

1. **lakes, ponds** : areas of water. Lakes are bigger and deeper than ponds.
2. **landscape** : everything that you can see when you look across an area of land. 'Landscape gardens' looked like the country around a house.
3. **the public** : (here) everybody in a country, not just one class of people.

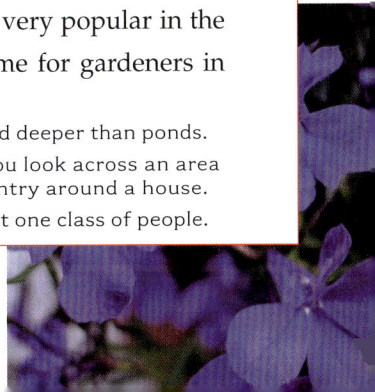

The Palm House at Kew Gardens.

1936, *In Your Garden*, and in 1955 the first television programme for gardeners, *Gardening Club*. Gardening programmes in the media are still very popular now.

Nearly half of British people say gardening is one of their hobbies. You can see this in British villages, where the gardens of cottages are small but full of flowers. Another example of the British love of gardens is the National Gardens Scheme. More than 3,300 ordinary people open their gardens to the public, who pay about three pounds for the visit. The money is given to charities: since it began in 1927 more than £20 million has been given to charities. [1]

Yet another example is the popularity of the Chelsea Flower Show, the most famous flower show in the world, started by the Royal Horticultural [2] Society in 1913. It takes place in Chelsea in London every year in May and lasts five days. A lot of gardens are created for the public to enjoy, and thousands of people come.

1. **charities** : organisations which collect money to help people who are ill or poor.
2. **Horticultural** : interested in horticulture (growing flowers, fruit and vegetables). The Royal Horticultural Society started in 1804.

1 Comprehension check

What does the text say about the following? Write down a few key words, then prepare to say a sentence about each of them.

1 Green spaces in the capital city
2 Gardens of big country houses
3 Fashions in the 18th century
4 Fashions in the 19th century
5 Elements of a typical garden
6 Gardening in the media
7 Gardening and charity
8 An important gardening show

2 Speaking

1 What are similarities and differences between gardens and gardening in Britain and in your country? Prepare a short talk on this.
2 A friend from abroad has asked to see a picture of a typical garden in your country. Find a picture and describe it.

▶▶ INTERNET PROJECT ◀◀

The Royal Botanic Gardens at Kew in the south of London are often called 'Kew Gardens'. Let's find out about them.
Connect to the Internet and go to www.blackcat-cideb.com. Insert the title or part of the title of the book into our search engine. Open the page for *The Secret Garden*. Click on the Internet project link. Go down the page until you find the title of this book and click on the relevant link for this project.

▶ Find out where Kew Gardens are, how to get there, the price and visiting times.
▶ Go to the interactive map. Click on the Palm House and find some details about this place.
▶ Go back to the interactive map and find two other places you would like to visit.
▶ Try to find something really strange: for example carnivorous plants, or the plant called Rafflesia Arnoldi…

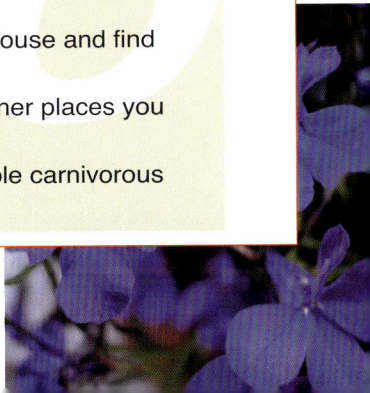

Before you read

1 **Listening**

PET

Listen to Chapter Four. For each question, put a tick (✓) in the correct box.

1 When Mary first saw Dickon he was playing

A ☐ a pipe.
B ☐ with two rabbits.
C ☐ with a squirrel.

2 Dickon had

A ☐ brown eyes.
B ☐ blue eyes.
C ☐ grey eyes.

3 Dickon brought Mary

A ☐ two rabbits and a squirrel.
B ☐ a pipe.
C ☐ some tools and seeds.

4 Dickon said that

A ☐ the plants and trees were dead.
B ☐ he already knew the garden.
C ☐ the garden was alive.

5 Mary thought that Mr Craven

A ☐ was frightening.
B ☐ looked sad and worried.
C ☐ had a crooked back.

6 Mary asked Mr Craven

A ☐ for some flowers.
B ☐ for a bit of garden.
C ☐ to meet Mrs Craven.

CHAPTER FOUR

Dickon

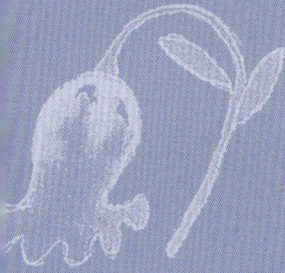

ne day Mary saw a boy sitting under a tree. He
seemed about twelve years old. He was playing a
pipe. Two rabbits and a squirrel [1] were near him.
They seemed to listen to the tune he was playing.

The boy got up carefully because he didn't want to frighten
the animals. He had blue eyes and a round, pink face.

'I'm Dickon,' he said to Mary. 'I've brought you the garden tools
and some flower seeds.'

Dickon had a kind, gentle smile and Mary felt that she knew
him quite well. She felt that if the wild animals could trust [2] him,
then she could trust him, too.

'Do you know about the secret garden?' asked Mary.

'I've heard about it,' Dickon answered, 'But I don't know where
it is.'

1. **squirrel** :
2. **trust** : believe he was honest and wouldn't hurt them.

The Secret Garden

'Come with me,' Mary said.

Mary was careful; she didn't want anyone to see them. She took Dickon through the door in the wall. Dickon was very surprised. 'This is a strange, pretty place,' he said. 'It's like being in a dream.'

Dickon looked around at all the plants and trees which Mary thought were dead. 'All of these will grow,' he said. 'There'll be flowers and roses everywhere in a few weeks.'

Dickon and Mary worked together to clear away weeds and dead wood. Mary didn't know anyone like Dickon. She tried to speak in a warm, friendly voice, like Dickon's and Martha's.

'Do you like me?' she asked.

'Yes, I do,' he laughed. 'The robin likes you, too.'

They continued working and Mary was sorry when it was time to go inside for lunch. She said goodbye to Dickon and ran into the house.

'I've met Dickon,' she told Martha.

'Do you like him?' asked Martha.

'Oh yes!' said Mary. 'He's very nice.'

That evening after dinner, Martha told Mary that Mr Craven was at home. 'He's going away again tomorrow, and he wants to see you first,' she said. When Mrs Medlock took Mary to meet him, Mary was a little afraid. She felt sure that she would not like Mr Craven and that he would not like her. But she found that Mr Craven wasn't really frightening, and that his back wasn't really crooked. His face was handsome, but he looked sad and worried. He asked Mary if there was anything that she would like. Mary asked for a bit of garden in which to grow her own flowers.

The Secret Garden

'Of course, you can take any bit that isn't used. You remind me of my wife. She loved gardens and flowers,' he said with a sad smile.

Mary was very happy. Now she could have the secret garden for herself!

'I can have my garden!' Mary cried to Martha. 'Mr Craven is very nice — but he's very sad.'

She ran to the garden. Dickon wasn't there but she found a note from him. It said, 'I'll come back.'

Later that night, Mary was woken up by the wind blowing around the house. She couldn't sleep, and as she lay in bed, she heard the crying noise again. 'That's not the wind,' she thought. 'I'm going to find out where that noise is coming from.'

Mary took a candle so that she could see in the dark corridors. Suddenly, she noticed a light from under one of the doors. The crying noise came from behind the door, and Mary knew that it was a child. She gently opened the door and saw a young boy lying on the bed, crying.

When the boy saw Mary, he stopped crying at once. 'Are you a ghost?' he asked. He looked very frightened.

'No, I'm Mary Lennox,' she answered. 'Who are you?'

Go back to the text

PET **1** **Comprehension check**

Read the questions below and for each question choose the correct answer — A, B, C or D.

1 What did Dickon bring for Mary?
- **A** [ ] seeds and tools
- **B** [ ] a key
- **C** [ ] a squirrel and two rabbits
- **D** [ ] a pipe

2 Where did Mary take Dickon?
- **A** [ ] out on the moor
- **B** [ ] inside the house
- **C** [ ] to the secret garden
- **D** [ ] to the robin's nest

3 What did Mary learn about the secret garden from Dickon?
- **A** [ ] that it had a door
- **B** [ ] that she had to pull the weeds out of the ground to make the flowers grow
- **C** [ ] that the plants and trees were not really dead
- **D** [ ] that it was Mr Craven's wife's garden

4 Mary spoke in a warm, friendly voice because
- **A** [ ] she didn't want to frighten the animals
- **B** [ ] she liked Dickon
- **C** [ ] the robin liked her
- **D** [ ] the sun was shining

5 When Mary finally met her uncle she discovered that
- **A** [ ] he did not really have a crooked back and he was handsome
- **B** [ ] he was going abroad
- **C** [ ] his wife died ten years earlier
- **D** [ ] he never went into the locked garden

6 What did Mary ask her uncle for?
- **A** [ ] permission to enter the secret garden
- **B** [ ] permission to go where she wanted in the house
- **C** [ ] some seeds and tools for her garden
- **D** [ ] an area of garden where she could grow her own flowers

49

PET ❷ Sentence transformation

Here are some sentences from the chapters you have read.
For each question, complete the second sentence so that it means the
same as the first, using no more than three words.

0 She heard nothing.
She ..didn't hear.................... anything.

1 Perhaps it's the key to the garden.
It .... be the key to the garden.

2 Mary was very pleased to see them and she kissed them.
Mary was .... to see them that she kissed them.

3 Go back to your room, or I'll tell Mr Craven that you refused to do what I told you.
If .... to your room, I'll tell Mr Craven that you refused to do what I told you.

4 He's going away tomorrow and he wants to see you first.
He wants to see you before .... tomorrow.

5 I'll wait until the rain stops before I decide what to do.
I'll decide what to do .... the rain stops.

PET ❸ Summary

Read the summary of the first four chapters of *The Secret Garden* and
choose the correct word for each space. For each question, mark the
letter next to the correct word — A, B, C or D.

Mary Lennox lived (**0**) ..D...... India, but when (**1**) .... of Mary's parents died during a terrible epidemic, she was sent to live with her uncle, Mr Craven, in Yorkshire. Mary arrived (**2**) .... London where Mr Craven's housekeeper, Mrs Medlock, was waiting (**3**) .... her. They travelled by train to Yorkshire. During the trip Mrs Medlock told Mary about her uncle. His wife was dead, and he was now an unpleasant man. The (**4**) .... morning the housemaid, a young girl named Martha, awakened Mary. She told Mary about her large family (**5**) .... lived on the moor, and about her brother Dickon, who loved animals. She also told her about a

50

walled garden that was locked up. Mary went out to look at the gardens. She found one walled garden without a door.

One evening after dinner Mary asked Martha to tell her (6) .... Mr Craven locked up the garden. She explained that his wife fell from a tree there, and died. As they were talking Mary thought she heard a child crying.

The next day in the garden, as Mary was watching a robin, she found a key. Then another day, the wind blew some ivy to one side and she saw a door. She opened the door with the key. She was then inside the locked garden.

Mary went to the garden every day. But she never told (7) .... about it until one day Dickon came to see her. He was so kind that she felt she could trust him. She took him to the garden.

That evening she met (8) .... uncle for the first time. He was going away and wanted to know if she wanted anything. She said she wanted a piece of garden where she could grow flowers. He told her that she could have any part of the garden that was unused.

That night Mary was woken up by the wind, and once again she heard a child crying. She decided to find (9) .... the truth. She left her room and finally found the room where the crying came (10) .... She opened the door, and inside she saw a young boy lying on a bed.

0	**A** into	**B** on	**C** by	**(D)** in
1	**A** both	**B** either	**C** together	**D** two
2	**A** in	**B** at	**C** to	**D** from
3	**A** for	**B** on	**C** by	**D** to
4	**A** after	**B** then	**C** last	**D** next
5	**A** which	**B** who	**C** whose	**D** those
6	**A** how	**B** why	**C** because	**D** what
7	**A** somebody	**B** nobody	**C** everybody	**D** anybody
8	**A** his	**B** her	**C** its	**D** hers
9	**A** out	**B** in	**C** over	**D** by
10	**A** of	**B** from	**C** out	**D** to

51

Before you read

1 **Listening**

PET

Listen to Chapter Five and for each question put a tick (✓) in the correct box.

1 Who is Colin?

    A ☐ Mary's cousin

    B ☐ Mr Craven's cousin

    C ☐ Mr Craven's nephew

2 Colin's father is afraid that

    A ☐ Colin will grow up to have a crooked back.

    B ☐ Mary will stare at Colin.

    C ☐ Colin will hate him.

3 Colin wants Mary

    A ☐ to go away.

    B ☐ not to look at him.

    C ☐ to stay and talk to him.

4 Everybody at Misselthwaite must do what Colin says because

    A ☐ if they don't he will send them away.

    B ☐ if they don't he will become ill.

    C ☐ if they don't he will become very angry.

5 How old is Colin?

    A ☐ eight

    B ☐ nine

    C ☐ ten

6 When Colin hears about the secret garden he becomes

    A ☐ sad.

    B ☐ excited.

    C ☐ angry.

CHAPTER FIVE

Colin

'm Colin' said the boy.

'Colin? I'm sorry, I still don't understand...' said Mary.

'I'm Colin Craven. Who are you?'

'I am Mary Lennox. Mr Craven is my uncle.'

'He's my father,' said the boy.

'Your father!' said Mary. 'No one told me he had a son! Then I must be your cousin.' Don't you know that I came to live here?'

'No,' he answered. 'No one told me.'

'Why?' asked Mary.

'Because I'm afraid that people will see me. I don't want people to see me and talk about me.'

'Why?' asked Mary. She felt more and more confused.

'Because I'm always ill, and I must stay in bed. The servants aren't allowed to talk about me. My father doesn't want anyone to talk about me to anyone. He's afraid I'll grow up [1] with a

---

1. **grow up** : become adult.

crooked back. My father doesn't want to see me because my mother died when I was born, and when he sees me he feels very sad. He thinks I don't know, but I do. He hates me.'

'He hates the garden, too, because she died,' said Mary.

'What garden?' asked Colin.

'Oh, just a garden she liked,' said Mary. 'Have you always been here?'

'Nearly always,' said Colin. 'If I go out, people look at me, and I hate it.'

'If you don't like people to see you,' Mary said, 'shall I go away?'

'Oh, no!' Colin replied quickly. 'You must stay and talk to me.'

Mary put her candle down on a table near the bed and sat on a chair. They talked for a long time. Colin wanted to know all about Mary and about her life at Misselthwaite. He told her how unhappy and lonely he was, even though he was given anything that he wanted.

'Everyone must do as I say,' Colin said. 'I'll be ill if they don't.'

'Do you think you will get well?' Mary asked.

'I don't think I will,' Colin answered. 'No one believes I will live until I grow up. But I don't want to die. When I think about it and I cry and cry.'

'I heard you crying before,' said Mary, 'but I didn't know who it was. Were you crying about that?'

Let's talk about something else,' said Colin. How old are you?'

'I'm ten, like you,' Mary said.

'How do you know I'm ten?' he asked.

'Because when you were born, your father locked the garden door and buried the key. And I know it was locked ten years ago,' Mary answered.

The Secret Garden

'What garden?' Colin asked.

'The garden Mr Craven hates,' said Mary, nervously. 'He locked the door. No one knows where he buried the key.'

'What's the garden like?' Colin asked.

'As I said, it was locked ten years ago,' Mary said, carefully. She didn't want him to know that she found it. But it was too late to be careful. Colin was very excited at the idea of a secret garden.

'I'll make them open the door,' he said.

'Oh, no!' cried Mary. 'Let's keep it a secret. If they open the door, it will never be a secret again. If we find the door one day, we can go inside and no one will know about it except us.'

'I would like that,' said Colin. 'I have never had a secret before. I think that you will be my secret too.'

Colin looked tired. 'Do you want me to go away now?' asked Mary.

'I would like to go to sleep before you leave me,' answered Colin.

Mary felt sorry for Colin and waited until he fell asleep. Then she took her candle and went quietly away.

Go back to the text

1 **Comprehension check**

Read the chapter again and answer the questions. Write out your answers.

1 Mary asked Colin why no one told him that she lived at Misselthwaite Manor. What was his reply?
2 Why was Colin afraid to go out?
3 Why did Colin think that his father hated him?
4 How did Mary know Colin's age?
5 Why didn't Mary want Colin to know that she found the secret garden?

2 **Possessive 's**

Use the possessive 's to show the relationship between the following people. Then rewrite each sentence using possessive pronouns.

0 Mr Lennox (Mary's father) and Colin

Mr Lennox was Colin's uncle. / Mr Lennox was his uncle.
Colin was Mr Lennox's nephew./ Colin was his nephew.

1 Mary and Mr Craven

....
....

2 Mrs Lennox (Mary's mother) and Colin

....
....

3 Mr Craven and Colin

....
....

4 Martha and Dickon

....
....

PET 3 Signs

Look at the text in each question. What does it say?
Mark the letter next to the correct explanation — A, B or C.

1 We advise mixing powder in water and waiting until water is blue before giving to patient

A ☐ Do not give the medicine to the patient without a glass of water.

B ☐ Put the powder in water. Wait for the water to turn blue, and then give it to the patient.

C ☐ Give the patient only blue powder.

2 *Mrs Medlock*
Prepare my suitcases for Thursday evening. I will be leaving Friday morning instead of Thursday as I thought. Mr Craven

A ☐ Mr Craven thinks he is leaving on Thursday evening.

B ☐ Mr Craven was going to leave on Thursday morning but now he is leaving a day later.

C ☐ Mr Craven wants to leave on Friday but he has to leave on Thursday.

3 Plant daffodil and crocus bulbs in late autumn or early winter, and not in the spring or summer, otherwise plants will not produce flowers.

A ☐ Daffodils and crocuses produce flowers only in early autumn.

B ☐ If the daffodil and crocus bulbs are planted in the spring or summer they will produce flowers.

C ☐ If the daffodil and crocus bulbs are planted in the autumn or early winter they will produce flowers.

4 *From Mrs Medlock to housemaid*
Clean Mr Craven's bedroom every day except if I tell you not to.

A ☐ Mrs Medlock will tell the housemaid if she must clean Mr Craven's room.

B ☐ The housemaid must clean Mr Craven's room only when Mrs Medlock tells her to do so.

C ☐ The housemaid must not clean Mr Craven's room only if Mrs Medlock tells her not to do so.

5   Dickon,
    I met Colin Craven. I am not going to tell him that we go inside the secret
    garden until I am sure I can trust him.
    Mary

A ☐ Colin wanted to know about the secret garden but
        Mary did not tell him anything about it.

B ☐ Mary does not trust Colin. That is why she did not tell
        him that she and Dickon have been inside it.

C ☐ When Mary feels that she can trust Colin she will tell
        him that she and Dickon go inside the secret garden.

Before you read

1 Listening

PET

**Listen to the beginning of Chapter Six and decide if each sentence is
correct or incorrect. If it is correct, put a tick (✓) in the box under A
for YES. If it is not correct, put a tick (✓) in the box under B for NO.**

		A YES	B NO
1	Martha was happy when Mary told her that she found Colin.	☐	☐
2	Colin once cried until he became ill because he thought a gardener was looking at him.	☐	☐
3	Colin thinks that the moor is a horrible place.	☐	☐
4	Colin always seemed frightened when he said that he was going to die.	☐	☐
5	Colin thinks that his father will be happy when he dies.	☐	☐
6	A famous doctor said that Colin should go out.	☐	☐

**Now read the beginning of Chapter Six and correct the incorrect
sentences.**

Wet Weather

ext morning, Mary told Martha about finding Colin. Martha was very upset. She thought that she could lose her job for allowing Mary to find Mr Craven's son.

'Don't worry,' said Mary. 'Colin was pleased to see me. He wants to see me every day.'

'Really! How did you do that? Did you use magic?' said Martha.

'What's the matter with him?' Mary asked.

Martha told Mary that Colin's father never allowed Colin to walk. His father thought that his back was weak. A famous doctor came to see him, and said that he would get strong if they didn't make a fuss of [1] him.

But Colin was still spoilt and allowed to do everything that he wanted.

---

1. **make a fuss of** : pay too much attention to.

'Colin thinks he is going to die,' said Mary.

'Mother says that he has no reason to live if he's closed up in his room all the time,' said Martha.

'It's good for me to be outside,' said Mary. 'Do you think that it would help Colin, too?'

'Oh, I don't know,' Martha said. 'He had a tantrum [1] when he was taken into the garden. He was upset because he thought one of the gardeners was looking at him. He cried until he felt ill.'

'If he ever gets angry with me, I won't go to see him again,' said Mary.

Martha went to see Colin and came back ten minutes later. She looked confused. 'You have used magic on him. He's not in bed. He's sitting on the sofa looking at his books. He wants to see you.'

Mary was happy to go and see Colin. 'Why are you looking at me like that?' asked Colin.

'I was thinking how different you are from Dickon,' said Mary.

'Who is Dickon?' asked Colin, 'What a strange name!'

Mary told him about Dickon. 'He's not like anyone else,' she said. 'All the animals on the moor love him. When he plays his pipe, they come to listen.'

'The moor must be a wonderful place,' said Colin. 'But I can't go there. I'm going to die.'

'How do you know that?' Mary asked. She felt a little angry. with Colin. He seemed to be pleased with the thought that he could die.

'Because everyone says I will die,' Colin replied. 'I think that my father will be pleased when I'm dead.'

---

1. **tantrum** : a bad-tempered explosion of anger.

'I don't believe that,' Mary said. 'That famous doctor was right. They shouldn't make a fuss of you; they should allow you to go out. If you see Dickon, you'll want to get well.'

Then Mary told Colin about Dickon's family, who had no money but were all healthy and happy.

It rained for a week, so Mary couldn't visit the garden. Because the weather was so bad, she spent most of her time with Colin. They read books and talked together, and for the first time Mary heard Colin laugh. Colin often talked about the secret garden, and wondered what was in it. Mary felt that she could not tell him her secret yet, so she still didn't tell him that she knew where the mysterious garden was.

'I'll wait until the rain stops before I decide what to do,' thought Mary.

On the day that the rain stopped, Mary woke up early and saw that the sunlight was shining through her window. She went quickly to the secret garden, and she found that Dickon was already there.

'I couldn't stay in bed on a morning like this,' he said. 'Look at the garden.' The new plants were starting to come through the earth. There were some purple, orange and gold crocuses. Mary was very pleased to see them, and she kissed them. The robin was building a nest. [1]

'We mustn't go too near,' Dickon said. 'If we don't frighten him, he'll stay here with us.'

Mary told Dickon that she found Colin the week before, when it was raining and she had to stay inside.

'If he comes out here in the garden, he'll forget that he's ill,' Dickon said. 'He'll be another child, looking at the flowers and animals, like us.'

When Mary went back to the house at the end of the day, Martha told her that Colin was angry because she didn't go to see him. Mary went to Colin's room.

'I won't allow that boy to come here if you stay with him instead of me,' Colin said.

'If you send Dickon away, I'll never come into this room again!' Mary replied.

'You're selfish!' [2] Colin said angrily.

'What about you?' Mary replied, even more angrily. 'You're the most selfish boy I know.'

'Well, I'm going to die!' Colin said.

'No, you're not!' Mary replied. 'You just say that to make

---

1. **nest** : place made by a bird to lay eggs in.

2. **You're selfish!** : You only think about yourself!

people feel sorry for you. But they don't feel sorry. You're too nasty.'[1]

Mary went to the door and then said, 'I was going to tell you all about Dickon and his fox and crow, but I won't now!' She slammed[2] the door behind her.

Later, when Mary remembered how lonely Colin was, she felt sorry for him.

'I'll go and see him tomorrow,' she thought. 'I'll go and sit with him.'

Later that night, Mary was woken up by the sound of screaming and crying. 'Colin is having one of his tantrums,' she thought.

She put her hands over her ears, but she couldn't block out the terrible noise.

'Someone should stop him!' she cried. 'He's so selfish he should be punished. He's woken up everyone in the house.'

She ran into Colin's room and shouted at him, 'Stop! I hate you! Everyone hates you! You'll scream until you die, and I hope that you do!'

1. **nasty** : unkind and unpleasant.
2. **slammed** : closed noisily.

Go back to the text

1 Comprehension check
Answer the questions.

1 Why did Colin have a temper tantrum the last time he was taken outside?
2 Why did Colin think that he was going to die?
3 How did Colin and Mary spend the time while it was raining?
4 How could Colin get well, according to Dickon?
5 Why did Colin get angry with Mary?

2 Mary's cousin Colin
Discuss these questions with a partner.

1 How is Colin similar to Mary when she first arrived at Misselthwaite Manor?
2 How does Mary's company change Colin?
3 Why do you think Colin has a temper tantrum in the middle of the night?
4 What do you think about Mary's reaction to that temper tantrum?

3 Mixed-up sentences
Here are six mixed-up sentences from the story. Put the words in their correct order.

1 very upset was Martha.
2 the garden Mary not visit could rained It so week for a.
3 a nest was robin building The.
4 time the Mary Colin for laugh heard first.
5 crying and Mary woken up sound of screaming was by the.
6 ran into shouted him at Colin's and room She.

4 **The characters**

Here are some adjectives that describe the characters in the story. Choose suitable adjectives for each character, and write them under the picture.

> old   handsome   selfish   kind   sad   unpleasant
> friendly   happy   grumpy   plain   rude

Mary

....
....

Martha

....
....

Ben

....
....

Colin

....
....

Mr Craven

....
....

Dickon

....
....

66

5 **What goes where?**

A   Martha is helping Mary choose some clothes to wear when she goes out to the garden. First label the articles of clothing.

1 ....

2 ....

3 ....

4 ....

B   Now complete the following sentences. The words you need are in the wordsquare.

N	H	G	E	S
T	E	M	L	D
E	A	C	H	N
E	D	N	K	A
F	U	S	R	H

1   She will wear the hat on her ....
2   She will wear the gloves on her ....
3   She will wear the scarf around her ....
4   She will wear the boots on her ....

Before you read

8 ❶ Listening

PET

Listen to the beginning of Chapter Seven. You will hear three conversations: two with Colin and Mary, and one with Mary and Dickon. For each question, fill in the missing information in the numbered space.

Colin and his back

Mary looked at Colin's back for (**1**) .... time.

She discovered that it was (**2**) .... hers.

What should be done for Colin

Dickon thinks they should take Colin out of the (**3**) ....

....

Colin learns about the garden

Colin says he is (**4**) ....
he got angry about Dickon.

Dickon is coming to see Colin with his (**5**) ....

Mary waited to tell Colin about the garden until she was sure she could (**6**) .... him.

❷ Reading pictures

Look at the pictures on pages 69 and 71 and answer the questions.

1   Who is in the pictures?

2   What is happening?

3   Where do you think they are going?

4   How do you think the story will end?

CHAPTER SEVEN

I Will Live
For Ever and Ever!

olin looked terrible. His face was red from crying, but Mary was too angry to worry about him. 'If you scream again, then I'll scream louder,' she told him.

'I can't stop,' Colin sobbed. [1] 'There's something wrong with my back. I'll have a crooked back, and then I'll die!'

'Turn over and let me look at your back,' Mary said. She looked at the poor, thin back for a long time. 'There's nothing wrong with it. Your back is as straight as mine,' she told him.

Colin stopped crying, and Mary sat by his bed, talking to him quietly until he fell asleep.

The next morning, Mary met Dickon in the garden, and she told him about Colin crying in the night.

1. **sobbed** : spoke while crying.

'The poor boy! We must get him out here,' said Dickon kindly.

'Yes, we must,' said Mary.

Mary went to see Colin later that day. She told him about Dickon and his squirrels, who were called Nut and Shell. Then Colin said, 'I'm sorry I said that I would send Dickon away. He seems a wonderful boy.'

'I'm pleased you said that,' said Mary, 'because he's coming to see you tomorrow, and he's bringing his animals.'

Colin suddenly looked happy. Mary decided to tell him her great secret.

'That's not all,' she said. 'There's something even better. I've found the door to the garden.'

Colin was very pleased. 'Then we can go in and find out what's inside,' he cried.

Mary waited for a moment, and then she told him the truth. 'I've been inside. That's why I could tell you so much about it. I couldn't tell you my secret until I was sure that I could trust you.'

The next day at breakfast, Colin told his nurse, 'A boy and his animals are coming to see me. Bring them straight up when they arrive.'

Soon afterwards, Mary heard bleating. [1]

'Can you hear that noise?' asked Mary.

'Yes. What is it?' asked Colin.

'That's Dickon's lamb,' she said. 'They're coming.'

Dickon came in. He was smiling. He carried a lamb and his little fox came in behind him. The squirrel sat on one shoulder and the crow on the other. The other squirrel was in his pocket.

Colin looked at him in surprise. Dickon gave the lamb to Colin and then gave him a bottle to feed it. The little boy was happy.

---

1. **bleating** : sound made by a lamb or sheep.

While he was feeding the lamb, Mary and Dickon talked about the garden and about the flowers that were growing there. Colin listened, and after some time he cried, 'I must see it all. I must see the secret garden!'

'Yes, of course you must,' said Mary, 'And you must see it now!'

They put Colin in his wheelchair, and Dickon pushed it along the garden paths. [1] Mary told Colin all about the places they passed on their way to the door to the secret garden.

---

1. **path** : line in the ground for walking along.

The Secret Garden

'Here's where I met Ben Weatherstaff,' she said, 'and this is where I saw the robin.' Then she said quietly to him, 'And this is the secret garden.'

Mary looked around to make sure that no one was watching, and then Dickon pushed the chair quickly inside. Colin looked at the trees and flowers. He listened to the sweet sound of the birds singing, and he felt the warm sun on his face. His pale skin started to become pink as he breathed in the good, fresh air. Then he cried out, 'I will be well. I will live for ever and ever!' That day, the world changed for Colin.

'It's been a wonderful day,' said Dickon.

'Yes it has,' replied Mary.

'I don't want this day to finish, but I'll come back every day,' Colin said.

Go back to the text

PET **1** **Comprehension check**

For each question, mark the letter next to the correct answer — A, B, C or D.

1 How did Mary get Colin to stop crying?
   A ☐ She became angry with him.
   B ☐ She sang him an Indian song.
   C ☐ She told him about Dickon's animals.
   D ☐ She looked at his back and told him that it was straight.

2 Dickon thought that it would be good for Colin if he
   A ☐ went to see his father.
   B ☐ went to see another doctor.
   C ☐ talked with Dickon's mother.
   D ☐ went out into the garden.

3 Colin forgot about his jealousy and decided he wanted to meet Dickon because
   A ☐ Dickon knew a lot about gardens.
   B ☐ Mary told him that she would never talk to him again if he did not meet Dickon.
   C ☐ Mary told him about Dickon's squirrels.
   D ☐ Dickon had a Yorkshire accent.

4 As Colin, Mary and Dickon walked to the secret garden, Mary told Colin about
   A ☐ how beautiful the secret garden was.
   B ☐ how she discovered that the secret garden was really alive.
   C ☐ all the things that happened to her in the gardens since her arrival.
   D ☐ how Mr Craven gave her permission to have her own garden.

5 That day in the secret garden Colin realised that
   A ☐ Dickon was actually a nice boy.
   B ☐ Mary was his best friend.
   C ☐ there was a secret garden.
   D ☐ he was going to have a life of his own.

73

I will be well! I will live for ever and ever!

We often use the expressions or words: **I think, I expect, perhaps, maybe, I am sure** with **will**,

I am sure that you will get well.   ***Perhaps** it **will rain** tomorrow.*

We use **will** or the negative **won't**:

1 when we decide to do something at the moment we are speaking: (You are looking at the menu in a restaurant) *I'll have a hamburger and French fries.*
2 when we offer to do something: (The phone rings but your mum is busy) *I'll answer the phone!*

We also use **will/won't** when we promise to do something: *I **won't tell** anybody about the secret garden, I promise.*

We use **going to to** talk about the future too. But it generally refers to something we have already decided to do and something we intend to do. *I **am going to work** as a gardener this summer.* (Mr Craven has said I can begin in June.)

2 *Going to* or *will*

Complete the sentences below with *going to* or *will* according to the context.

0 Mary: Why have you got that bucket of water?
   Ben: I <u>am going to water</u> (water) the rose bushes.

1 Mother: Has Mary decided about next year?
   Martha: Yes, Mother. She .... (study) with a governess, but most of the time she .... (work) in her garden with Colin and Dickon.

2 Jamie: Carol, I lent you my bicycle a week ago!
   Carol: Oh, you're right! I'm sorry. I .... (bring) it back this afternoon.

3 I've done the shopping. This evening .... (cook) a really special meal.

4 Sam: No, you can't use my computer I'm sure you .... (break) it.
   Jerry: Please, Sam I .... (break) it. You can trust me!

5 Martha: Mary, tomorrow is a holiday, and I .... (see) my mother and family.

74

Mary: Really? Tell your mother that I love the skipping rope.

Martha: Sure, I .... (*tell*) her.

3 Where are the rabbits?

There are six rabbits hiding in the secret garden. Using one of the following prepositions, work with a partner to say where the rabbits are hidden. See which pair can be first to find all the rabbits:

on   under   behind   in front of   on top of   next to

The following words will help you: flower pot   sunflower   hedge

1   There is a rabbit... ....

2   ....

3   ....

4   ....

5   ....

6   ....

Before you read

1 **Listening**

PET

Listen to the beginning of Chapter Eight.
For each question, put a tick (✓) in the correct box.

1 Who discovered Mary, Dickon and Colin in the garden?

A ☐ Mrs Medlock

B ☐ Mr Craven

C ☐ Ben Weatherstaff

2 What did Colin do when he saw that person?

A ☐ He told the person to go away.

B ☐ He told Mary and Dickon to run away.

C ☐ He showed the person that he could stand up.

3 What did Colin think made him strong?

A ☐ his medicine

B ☐ the magic of the garden

C ☐ his friendship with Mary and Dickon

4 As soon as he was really strong he wanted to

A ☐ go into his father's study and show him that he was a normal, healthy boy.

B ☐ leave Misselthwaite and look for his father.

C ☐ run away with Dickon and Mary, and never return to Misselthwaite.

5 It was not easy to keep a secret that Colin was no longer ill because

A ☐ Ben Weatherstaff saw Colin walking.

B ☐ Dickon told Martha and Martha was not good at keeping secrets.

C ☐ people could see from Colin's appearance that he was becoming healthier.

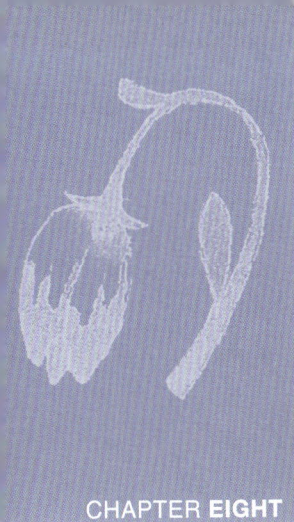

CHAPTER EIGHT

Magic

f course you will,' said Dickon. 'You'll soon be able to walk and work in the garden.'

But suddenly, Ben Weatherstaff's angry face looked down at them from the top of the wall. 'What are you doing in there,' he shouted angrily at Mary. Then he saw Colin, and his mouth opened in astonishment. [1]

'Do you know who I am?' Colin asked.

'Yes, of course I do,' Ben answered. 'You're the poor boy who is always ill.'

Colin sat up angrily. 'There's nothing wrong with me. I'll show you!' he cried. He pulled himself up out of his chair, and with Dickon's help he stood up straight and tall. 'Look at me,' he shouted at Ben. 'Just look at me!'

'You dear boy,' said Ben, and he started crying because he was so happy.

---

1. **astonishment** : great surprise.

77

The Secret Garden

Colin stayed standing. Suddenly, he stopped feeling afraid. 'I'm not afraid any more!' he cried. 'It's the magic of the secret garden. The magic that made all the plants grow strong has made me grow strong, too.'

That evening, when Colin was sitting with Mary, he was quiet. 'I'm not going to be a poor, sad boy any more. If I believe that I'll be strong and well, then the magic will make it happen.'

The next day, when the children went into the garden, Colin told Dickon and Mary to watch him. 'I'm going to show you that the magic has made me well,' he said.

Carefully, taking a few steps at a time, Colin walked around the garden. He looked very happy.

'Please keep this a secret,' he said. 'When I can walk and run really well, I'll walk into my father's study and say, "Here I am, as well and strong as any boy in Yorkshire."'

It was not easy to keep Colin's secret. The magic garden made Colin's eyes shine and his pale face become pink. Each day, Colin and Mary did exercises to make them strong, and soon they were happier and healthier. Mary looked pretty and Colin didn't look ill any more. Everyone who knew them was surprised at the change.

At the time that the secret garden made its magic for Colin, Mr Craven was travelling in Europe. He was trying to run away from his sadness but nothing could comfort him.

But one day, while he was walking in Austria, he sat down by a river and felt his mind and his body start to relax. The gentle sound of the running water filled him with peace, and suddenly he felt both healthy and happy.

Feeling better, he continued his journey to Italy. One night he fell asleep while sitting by Lake Como and dreamed about his

wife's garden and Misselthwaite Manor. The dream made him decide to return home at once. As soon as he arrived home he went to the garden.

As he walked slowly towards the door of the secret garden, all his sadness came back to him. He wondered how he could find the key to the garden, and then he heard laughter from the other side of the wall.

Then the door opened and a boy ran out. He was a tall, handsome boy, and Mr Craven looked at him, unable to speak.

Colin stood still and looked at his father in surprise. Then he said, 'Father, I'm Colin, your son. You can't believe it, but it's true.'

Colin took his father into the garden and told him how the magic made the flowers and trees grow, and made him grow strong and healthy.

Mr Craven thought that it was a wonderful story. He sat down next to Mary, Dickon and the animals and talked and laughed for the first time in ten years. He was very proud of his happy, healthy son.

'Now there will be no more secrets,' said Colin. 'I will never need my wheelchair again. I will walk with you, Father.'

They all stood up and walked back to the house. Mrs Medlock and Martha watched in astonishment as Mr Craven happily walked across the lawn. Next to him, with his head up high and his eyes full of laughter, walked Colin. He was as strong and well as any boy in Yorkshire!

Go back to the text

1 Comprehension check
Answer the following questions.

1 What did Ben do when he saw Colin stand?

2 Why was Mr Craven not often at Misselthwaite Manor?

3 What happened to Mr Craven by a river in Austria?

4 Why did he decide to come back home?

5 What was Mr Craven thinking about when he finally saw Colin again?

6 What did Mr Craven do for the first time in many years when he was with Colin again?

2 Think about the story

1 Look up the meaning of the surname of Colin and his father.

2 Do you think the author chose it on purpose? Why or why not?

3 The magic of the garden
A Say how the following people and things helped Mary become a happy little girl.

1 Ben Weatherstaff	5 The Yorkshire weather
2 Martha	6 The robin
3 Martha's mother	7 The secret garden
4 Dickon	

B Say how the following people and things helped Colin.

1 Mary

2 Dickon

3 The secret garden

T: GRADE 5

4 Speaking: transport

When Mary arrives in England she travels first by train and then by carriage. Bring to class a picture of a different type of transport and use the following questions to help you talk about it.

1 Is it a modern method of transport?
2 Was it used in the past?
3 How many people can ride on it at the same time?
4 Is it considered a fast method of transport?
5 How many other methods of transport can you think of?

5 Writing a letter

The years have passed and Mary has grown up and left Misslethwaite Manor. She receives a letter from a friend who asks her about her arrival in England from India:

You never told me about the time after your arrival in England but I know you changed a lot. What caused the change?

Now write your letter in about 100 words. Include the following information:

• what you were like when you arrived
• how you found the secret garden
• how you discovered Colin
• who and what changed you into a happy young girl

You can begin like this:

Dear Jane,

Your letter brought back memories of a time in my childhood which changed my life. When I arrived at Misselthwaite Manor from India...

6 **Word game**

Complete the crossword puzzle. It contains words from the entire book. Some of them can be found in the footnotes, but not all of them.

Across

1 Someone who is usually well is ....

5 If your tooth hurts you have ....

7 Not straight. (Colin's back was not ....)

9 A baby sheep.

11 Somebody who only thinks about himself is ....

12 A spirit, a phantasm.

15 'Ayah' is the Indian word for this English word.

16 Peas, carrots, potatoes and cucumbers are ....

18 The most important woman servant in a house.

21

23 Nut and Shell were the names of Dickon's ....

26 Mrs Medlock said that the .... was miles and miles of empty land.

28 If you believe that a person will not hurt you and is good, then you .... that person.

29 Instruments for working are ....

32 Great surprise.

33 What new plants grow from.

Down

2 If you .... a door, you close it with a key.

3 The area in northern England where *The Secret Garden* takes place.

4 the most important man servant in a house.

6 Feeling shy and ashamed.

8 Mary's cousin.

10 Chair with wheels.

13 Make happy. Give pleasure to.

14 'This' is used for things near us, and '........' is used for things far from us.

17

19 A wild animal that looks like a small dog (Dickon had one as a pet).

20 Sound made by a lamb or a sheep.

22 Passages in a building.

24 A boy or girl who is allowed to do everything he/she wants will become ....

25 'It is none of your ....' means 'This is private and does not concern you'.

27 A beautiful little bird with an orange breast, and Ben's only friend.

30 Ask yourself, be surprised.

31 Line in the ground for walking along.

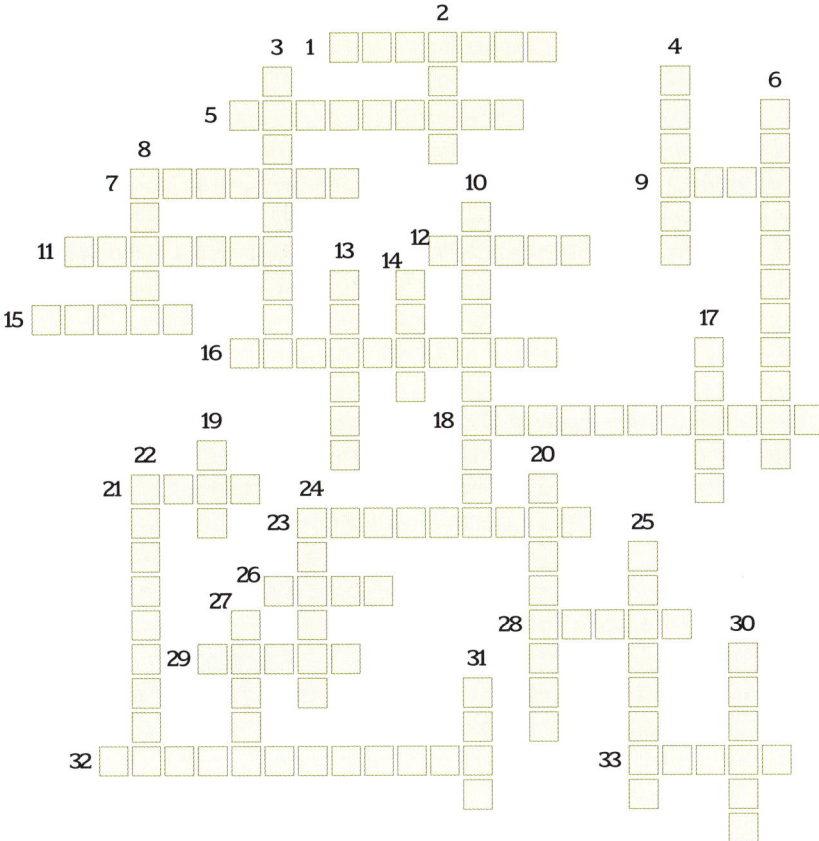

7 **A fairy tale**

What parts of *The Secret Garden* are like a fairytale? Now read this 'fairytale version' of *The Secret Garden* and say:

- who the princess is
- who the good fairy is
- who the elf is
- what the 'sweet, sleepy land' is
- what the 'lovely land of roses and fruit trees' is

- what the evil spirit is
- who the tree fairy is
- what the magic spell is
- what the castle is

Once upon a time there was a princess who lived in a sweet sleepy land where she had everything she wanted. But one day an evil spirit came and killed everyone in the kingdom except her. The princess ran away from the evil spirit. She travelled over vast seas until she came to a castle, where there lived a king and a prince. But the king and the prince were unhappy: the king walked about dreaming of his dead queen, and the prince lay asleep dreaming of his own death. Then one morning the princess awoke to see a good fairy standing by her bed. This good fairy told the princess that there was a magic spell to bring happiness. 'Where exactly?' asked the princess. But the good fairy smiled and said not a word. The princess left the king's palace and searched for days and days until she heard a sweet, magical song. She looked up and there was a little tree fairy all dressed in orange sitting in a tree. The tree fairy lead the princess through a door to a lovely land of roses and fruit trees. Then it disappeared. The princess was surprised and a little frightened but then she heard laughter. There in front of her was an elf. 'So,' said the elf, 'you want to know how to make the magic spell which brings happiness? Well, you will find the ingredients in the wind, the rain, the sun and scent of flowers.' After many days of hard work, she made enough of this magic spell. She went to the sleeping prince and just as she was about to place some of the spell on him a gust of wind came. The wind blew the spell onto the prince, onto the king and onto everything else in the castle. So it was that the prince, the princess and the king and all the people in the castle lived happily ever after.

▶▶▶ **INTERNET** PROJECT ◀◀◀

The North York Moors National Park is an area like that described in *The Secret Garden*.

Use one of the major search engines, or the site suggested by your teacher to find out:

▶ Where it is

▶ What you can do there

▶ When the best time to see the heather in bloom is

▶ Some myths and legends of the area

▶ The wild plants and animals that live in the park

North York Moors National Park – Discover This Special Place

NORTH YORK MOORS NATIONAL PARK   Search: [   ] ▶

| HOME | DISCOVER THE PLACE | AUTHORITY SERVICES | PLANNING | LEARNING ZONE | ONLINE SHOP |

Celebrating more than 50 years of being a National Park

What makes this a special place?

The North York Moors National Park is one of the finest landscapes in Britain. Miles of stunning heather, towering sea cliffs, secluded beaches and grassy dales give it a character all of its own. Discover wildlife, historic buildings, archaeology, ancient woodlands and picturesque villages. This site will help you make the most of your visit.

Find out how the North York Moors National Park Authority cares for this special place and our commitment to providing the highest quality service for locals and visitors.

National Park shop
SHOP ONLINE TODAY ▶

What's on ▶
Lots to see & do in & around the Park!

Latest news
▸ Help Improve Access to the National Park
▸ Edge Award Success
[...and more news]

MEET LAGOPUS IN THE **FUN ZONE**

Welcome: ▸ Welkom ▸ Bienvenue ▸ Willkommen ▸ Benvenuti

Discover The Place	**Authority Services**	**Planning**	**Learning Zone**
All you need to know to enjoy a winter break in the North York Moors National Park. How to get there... Where to stay... Public Transport... What to see... Activities... Events... and what makes it special	What the North York Moors National Park Authority does, why and how. Conservation, Recreation, Advice. Our Service to you. Our Members and Staff. Meetings and Agendas.	How the North York Moors National Park Planning system works ... Who's Who ... Planning Applications ... Policies and Plans ... Planning Advice ... Meetings and Agendas	School and group visits, Projects for schools, Facts and figures, Downloadable reports, plans and other publications

Copyright © North York Moors National Park Authority | **Site map** | **Contact us** | Designed and developed by **imaginet**

Then look at some of the photos and decide whether you think the moors are miles and miles of empty land, or a place full of busy and beautiful life.

The Rich and Poor
in Victorian Times

We have seen from *The Secret Garden* that there were many differences in Victorian times between the lives of rich people and the lives of poor people. Now, you are going to read about two children who have very different lives.

Charlotte's Story

My name is Charlotte. I am ten years old. I live in a very big house in the country. There are a lot of rooms in our house for me and my family, and there are also a lot of rooms for our servants. We have servants to cook, clean the house, look after us children, do the gardening and look after the horses. I have two younger sisters called Elizabeth and Julia, and one brother who is called Edward. Edward is thirteen. He goes to boarding school and only comes home for the holidays. My father is busy all day looking after the land [1] around our home. He owns a lot of farms which he rents [2] to other people. He likes riding horses and visiting his friends. My mother doesn't work, but she is busy some of the day looking after the house and telling the servants what to do. She plays the piano very well, and paints pictures of our house and the gardens. She also teaches Elizabeth and Julia to read and write. I have a governess to teach me my lessons. She lives in the house with us, and she takes me for a walk each day.

---

1. **land** : (here) open area of fields and woods.
2. **rent** : allow people to use for money.

Sympathy (1877) by Briton Rivière. The girl is sad, but she gets sympathy from her pet dog. Sentimental paintings were popular in Victorian times.

I like going out in the carriage with my family to visit friends and relations. Sometimes, as a special treat, we go to London on the train to see a play at the theatre.

We children are never allowed to go out without an adult. We are not allowed to play with the children in the village near our house, and we only meet the village people at Christmas, when we give presents of food and clothes to poor people. We see other people at church each Sunday, but we sit apart from them.

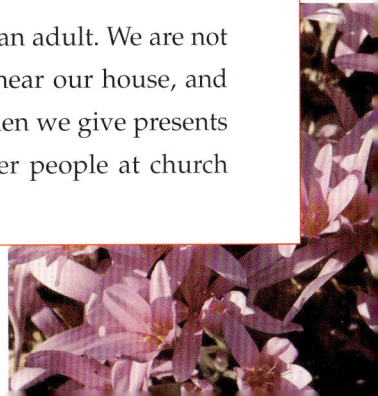

Clothes for upper class children, from the French fashion magazine
Le moniteur del la mode (*c*. 1880).

I like being rich because I live in a beautiful house and wear nice clothes. Sometimes, though, I feel sad because I have no one to play with except for my brother and sisters.

① **Comprehension check**

You are Charlotte. Answer these questions.

1   Where do you live?
2   How many brothers and sisters have you got?
3   Do you go to school?
4   What work does your father do?
5   What work does your mother do?
6   Who cooks and cleans in your house?
7   How do you travel to see your friends and relations?
8   Do you go out to play with other children?
9   Do you like being rich?

Sara's Story

My name is Sara. I am nine years old. I live in a small cottage in the country. It is really small: it has got one living room and two bedrooms. I have got three sisters and two brothers. We all sleep in one room. My father works on a farm. He gets up very early in the morning, before it is light in the winter. He looks after the farm animals and works in the fields. My mother works hard. She gets up very early, too, to bake [1]

A farm boy scaring the crows away from the crop by shouting and using wooden clackers (*c.* 1850).

bread for the family. There is no water in the house, so we older children have to get it from a well. [2]

The boys help father in the fields. They help to frighten the birds away, to stop them from eating the crops. We girls help mother in the house. We wash the clothes, bring in wood for the fire and we clean the house. There is no school in the village, but mother can read a little, and she teaches the little children when she is not too tired. The only lights we have come from candles.

Mother and father both work very hard, but we have very little

1. **bake** : cook in the oven.
2. **well** : a hole made in the ground from which to get water.

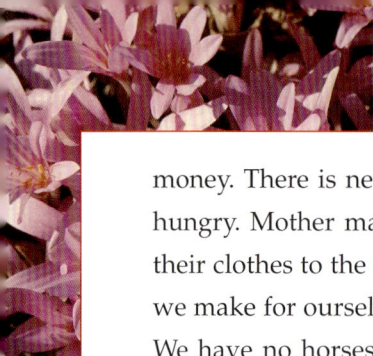

money. There is never enough food to eat and we always go to bed hungry. Mother makes all our clothes, and the big children pass on their clothes to the little ones. We have no toys, except for things that we make for ourselves. If we want to go anywhere, we have to walk. We have no horses to ride, and we have never been on a train. On Sundays we walk to church.

I like playing in the fields with my brothers and sisters, and with other children from the village. We like taking off our shoes and walking in the stream. In summer, we take home flowers for our

Young Gleaners Resting by a Stile (*c*. 1880) by Myles Birkett Foster.
After the crop was collected gleaners had to look for any plants or grain that were not collected. Victorian paintings of country scenes were often romantic, not realistic.

mother, and we pick wild berries [1] to eat after our dinner. Sometimes, before we go to bed, father tells us stories about what he did when he was a boy. Mother sings songs to help the little children to go to sleep.

I like living in a big family and I am really happy when I play with my brothers and sisters. But I would like to have more food to eat, and nice clothes to wear.

1 Comprehension check
Now pretend you are Sara, and answer these questions.

1   What kind of house do you live in?
2   Do you have your own bedroom?
3   How many children live in your house?
4   What work does your father do?
5   Do you have any servants?
6   Who does the cleaning and cooking?
7   How do you travel?
8   Do you ever play with Charlotte?
9   Do you get enough food to eat?

2 Speaking
Are there any advantages in the way Sara lives? Are there any disadvantages in the way Charlotte lives?

3 Writing
Write two biographies about a rich child and a poor child who live now. They can live in your country, or you can choose another place. Write about 100 words for each child.

1.   **berries** : small fruit, such as strawberries and blackberries.

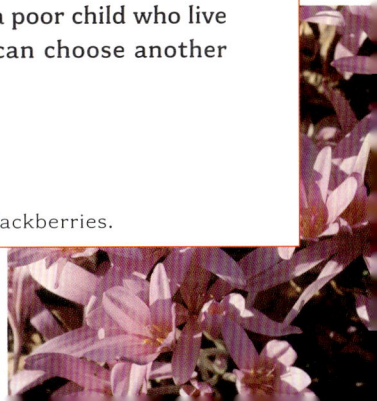

1 Characters

Of which of the people A-G are the following sentences true?

A Mary Lennox   B Martha   C Martha's mother

D Dickon   E Mr Craven   F Colin

G Ben Weatherstaff

Who...

travelled to forget about the past?	0	E
had a mother who was very beautiful and loved parties?	1	....
knew how to make children grow strong?	2	....
knew how to make plants grow strong?	3	....
knew how to make wild animals grow strong?	4	....
had only one friend in the world?	5	....
had no friends until he/she met a robin?	6	....
was spoilt because no one wanted him/her to have temper tantrums and get ill?	7	....
was spoilt because no one wanted him/her to have temper tantrums and disturb her mother?	8	....
often cried during the night'?	9	....
came home because of a dream?	10	....
discovered that Colin, Dickon and Mary played in the secret garden?	11	....
was sure that he/she had no future?	12	....
grew stronger as the plants began growing in the spring?	13	....
grew stronger among the plants of the spring?	14	....
thought the secret garden was like a dream?	15	....
thought the secret garden was dead when he/she first saw it?	16	....
thought the secret garden was magical?	17	....
had a mother who was very beautiful and loved gardens?	18	....
had a father who never saw him/her because he was too busy with work?	19	....
had a father who never saw him/her because he was too busy with his sadness?	20	....

2 Comprehension check

Answer the following questions.

1   How did Mary discover that her parents were dead?

2   What did Mary find surprising about Martha when they first met?

3   Why did Ben say that he and Mary were similar?

4   How did Mary first realise that perhaps there was another child in the house?

5   Why, according to Martha, did no one like Mary?

6   How did Mary find the door to the secret garden?

7   What did Colin think Mary was when he first saw her?

8   Why did Colin think that his father hated him?

9   How did Mary know how old Colin was?

10   What did a famous doctor say about Colin and his back?

11   How did Mary treat Colin when he had temper tantrums?

12   What did Colin want to do as soon as he could walk and run like other boys?

13   What was the first thing Mr Craven did when he returned from Austria?

This reader uses the **EXPANSIVE READING** approach, where the text becomes a springboard to improve language skills and to explore historical background, cultural connections and other topics suggested by the text.

The new structures introduced in this step of our **READING & TRAINING** series are listed below. Naturally, structures from lower steps are included too. For a complete list of structures used over all the six steps, see *The Black Cat Guide to Graded Readers*, which is also downloadable at no cost from our website, www.blackcat-cideb.com or www.cideb.it. The vocabulary used at each step is carefully checked against vocabulary lists used for internationally recognised examinations.

Step **Two** B1.1

All the structures used in the previous levels, plus the following:

Verb tenses
Present Perfect Simple: indefinite past with *yet, already, still*; recent past with *just*; past action leading to present situation
Past Perfect Simple: in reported speech

Verb forms and patterns
Regular verbs and most irregular verbs
Passive forms with *going to* and *will*
So / neither / nor + auxiliaries in short answers
Question tags (in verb tenses used so far)
Verb + object + full infinitive (e.g. *I want you to help*)
Reported statements with *say* and *tell*

Modal verbs
Can't: logical necessity
Could: possibility
May: permission
Might (present and future reference): possibility; permission
Must: logical necessity
Don't have to / haven't got to: lack of obligation
Don't need to / needn't: lack of necessity

Types of clause
Time clauses introduced by *when, while, until, before, after, as soon as*
Clauses of purpose: *so that; (in order) to* (infinitive of purpose)